Rancho
La Brea:

Science Series 31
Natural History Museum
of Los Angeles County

**Treasures
of the
Tar Pits**

Contributors

William A. Akersten
Curator of Pleistocene Terrestrial
Vertebrates
Natural History Museum
of Los Angeles County

Kenneth E. Campbell, Jr.
Curator of Fossil Birds
Natural History Museum
of Los Angeles County

John M. Harris
Chief Curator, Earth Sciences Division
Natural History Museum
of Los Angeles County

George T. Jefferson
Assistant Curator,
Rancho La Brea Section
George C. Page Museum
of La Brea Discoveries

James P. Quinn
Curatorial Assistant
Natural History Museum
of Los Angeles County

Christopher A. Shaw
Curatorial Assistant
George C. Page Museum
of La Brea Discoveries

Camm C. Swift
Associate Curator of Fishes
Natural History Museum
of Los Angeles County

Rancho La Brea:

Treasures of the Tar Pits

edited by
John M. Harris
and
George T. Jefferson

Natural History Museum
of Los Angeles County

Cover: Three life-size fiberglass reproductions of mammoths at the Lake Pits in front of the George C. Page Museum of La Brea Discoveries are a familiar sight to Los Angeles residents. The Lake Pit is the remnant of an asphalt quarry first mined by the Mexicans early in the nineteenth century.

Natural History Museum of Los Angeles County
Los Angeles 90007

©1985 by The Natural History Museum Foundation.
All Rights Reserved.
Published 1985.
Printed in Hong Kong
93 92 91 90 89 88 87 86   5   4   3   2   1

ISBN 0-938644-19-X
LC 85-61427

Designed by Renée Cossutta and Dana Levy (Perpetua Press)
Project Coordination by Robin A. Simpson
Typeset by Continental Typographics
Printed by Yu Luen Offset, Hong Kong
Distributed by the University of Washington Press
P.O. Box C50096
Seattle, WA 98145

Contents

Foreword

Fossils from the world-famous Rancho La Brea deposits, which Los Angeles residents call "the La Brea Tar Pits," were among the specimens in the collections when the Natural History Museum of Los Angeles County first opened in 1913. The museum was later given the responsibility for administering the 23-acre Hancock Park, the most richly fossiliferous portion of the Rancho La Brea deposits. Today, the extensive collections from Rancho La Brea are stored and featured in impressive exhibits in the George C. Page Museum of La Brea Discoveries in Hancock Park; this beautiful new museum is a satellite facility of the Natural History Museum.

The fossils from the Rancho La Brea deposits, which provide a detailed picture of life in North America during the closing phases of the last great Ice Age, have been the subject of many scientific and popular articles. Until now, the best available general description of the site and its fossils has been Dr. Chester Stock's *Rancho La Brea: A Record of Pleistocene Life in California*; written in 1930, the book was revised six times over the next three decades as knowledge of the Rancho La Brea fossils grew. New excavations and further studies in recent years have added dramatically to the diversity of animal and plant fossils known from the deposit. The abundance of new information about the fossils necessitated the compilation of the present book.

Rancho La Brea: Treasures of the Tar Pits was prepared by the staff and scientific associates of the Natural History Museum and Page Museum. The book explains how the asphalt deposits were formed, how the fossils came to be preserved, and how they were later discovered and excavated. Each major group of fossils is described, illustrated, and placed in context. The result is an introduction to a unique natural resource and a window into the life of the past.

Craig C. Black, Director
Natural History Museum
of Los Angeles County

Part 1

Introduction

Within the City of Los Angeles, only 7 miles west of the civic center, lies one of the world's richest deposits of "Ice Age" fossils. These provide an incredibly complete record of the different sorts of plants and animals that lived in the Los Angeles Basin between 4,000 and 40,000 years ago. Ranging in size from mammoth skeletons to fossils that may only be seen with the aid of a microscope, this ecologically diverse sample of past life includes diatoms, pollen, seeds, leaves and wood, clam and snail shells, insects and spiders, fish, frogs and toads, snakes and turtles, birds, and mammals—in all, more than 565 species.

The asphalt-rich sediments in which the fossils were preserved are known as the Rancho La Brea deposits. One hundred and fifty years ago, the area was part of a Mexican land grant called Rancho La Brea ("the tar ranch"). Here *muchos pantamos de brea* (extensive bogs of tar) were first recorded by the Spanish explorer Gaspar de Portola in 1769. The asphalt from this locality has been used by man since prehistoric times, but its treasure trove of fossils was only recognized just over a hundred years ago.

More than 100 excavations have been made at Rancho La Brea since the early 1900s, and most of the recovered fossils are now housed in the George C. Page Museum of La Brea Discoveries, located in Hancock Park at the very center of this unique deposit. This book discusses the historic, prehistoric, and geologic record of the area often called "the La Brea Tar Pits." Let it be your introduction to the discovery and diversity of Ice Age life in southern California.

A crew from the Southern California Academy of Sciences works on the north side of the Lake Pit in one of the first scientific excavations of Rancho La Brea deposits, circa 1910. The Hancock ranch house can be seen in the background.

History of Rancho La Brea

The naturally occurring asphalt deposits in which the Rancho La Brea fossils were preserved have been of local cultural and economic importance for a considerable period of time. For thousands of years the local Chumash and Gabrielino Indians, like others along the California coast, used the sticky asphalt as a glue for mending broken implements, hafting knives, and securing decorative shell inlay work on various ceremonial and household items. Asphalt was also used for waterproofing baskets and for caulking plank canoes. More recently, the asphalt was used as roofing tar by the inhabitants of the nearby Pueblo de Nuestra Señora la Reina de los Angeles. Indeed, the 1828 Rancho La Brea land grant stipulated that the people were to have unrestricted right to carry away as much *brea* as they needed for their personal use.

During the nineteenth century, the *brea* was mined commercially for between $13 and $16 per ton and used as far away as San Francisco. The occasional bones that were encountered during mining were regarded as the remains of unfortunate cattle and birds that had somehow become entangled in the asphalt. The true antiquity and importance of the fossils was not noted until 1875 when Major Henry Hancock,

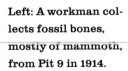

Left: A workman collects fossil bones, mostly of mammoth, from Pit 9 in 1914.

Right: Hundreds of thousands of fossil bones excavated from Rancho La Brea between 1913 and 1915 were identified, cataloged, and stored in the basement of the Natural History Museum.

owner of the Rancho, presented the large canine tooth of a saber-toothed cat to Professor William Denton of the Boston Society of Natural History. The first scientific investigations were made from 1901 to 1905 by W.W. Orcutt, a prominent Los Angeles geologist. During the ensuing decade, parties from Los Angeles High School (led by J.Z. Gilbert), Los Angeles Normal School (now the University of California at Los Angeles), the University of California at Berkeley, the University of Southern California, and the Southern California Academy of Sciences all excavated and collected at the site.

In 1913, Captain G. Allan Hancock gave the County of Los Angeles the exclusive right to excavate at Rancho La Brea for a period of two years. After first using dynamite to remove solidified caps of oxidized surface asphalt, the Natural History Museum staff carefully unearthed more than three-quarters of a million bones during this time. In May 1915, Captain Hancock officially donated the collection of fossils taken from the Rancho La Brea excavations to the museum and shortly thereafter offered the twenty-three acres of Rancho La Brea to the County of Los Angeles with the proviso that the scientific features of the fossil deposits be preserved and adequately exhib-

Parts of a basket and stone mortar have been glued together with asphalt; the Indians also used asphalt as a glue in decorative shell inlay work.

4

G. Allan Hancock (1875–1965). Courtesy of Allan Hancock Foundation.

ited. The area was subsequently renamed Hancock Park as a fitting memorial to the man who had contributed so much to the preservation of these important fossils.

Key Figures in the Study of Rancho La Brea Fossils

G. Allan Hancock

Captain Hancock, who inherited the major portion of Rancho La Brea from his parents in 1913, was a businessman, railroadman, navigator, pilot, rancher, marine scientist, musician, and patron of the arts. He encouraged the interest of the Natural History Museum in the fossils and made it possible for this unique scientific resource to be preserved for posterity. The extensive collection of fossils retrieved from Rancho La Brea between 1913 and 1915 is now known as the Hancock Collection.

Chester Stock

Chester Stock attended the University of California at Berkeley from 1910 to 1917. There he studied under Dr. John C. Merriam, who conducted excavations at Rancho La Brea from 1912 to 1913. Stock participated in these excavations and had published six papers on fossil ground sloths from Rancho La Brea by the time he was awarded his doctorate in 1917. From 1918 to 1949, Dr. Stock held a part-time appointment with the Natural History Museum while serving on university faculties, first at Berkeley and later at the California Institute of Technology. He published the first comprehensive account of the Rancho La Brea fossils in 1930 and later revised this classic monograph five times to keep pace with new information resulting from his research and that of others. He became Head of the Science Division at the museum in 1949; at the time of his death a year later he had supervised the construction of the Observation Pit structure and the preparation of the short-faced bear and Harlan's ground sloth statues and was preparing plans for the landscaping and construction of a geology museum for Hancock Park.

5

Chester Stock (1892–1950).

George C. Page (b. 1901).

George C. Page

George C. Page was a farm boy who at the age of 16 moved to California from Nebraska with just $2.30 in his pocket. In 1918, after a year of thrift and hard work, he opened his first store, selling gift packs of assorted fruits; this grew into the Mission Pak Company, which made him a millionaire. He has been a pioneer developer of some of the nation's first industrial parks and a civic-minded benefactor providing major donations to both public and private institutions. His early fascination with the unique La Brea asphalt deposits prompted him in 1973 to offer to build an innovative and spectacular museum on the site. Construction began in 1975, and the Page Museum of La Brea Discoveries was dedicated and opened to the public on April 13, 1977.

Geologic time scale showing, as is conventional, the most recent time at the top. The extinct vertebrate species from Rancho La Brea have been used to define an interval of time called the Rancholabrean Land Mammal Age. Although the fossils from Rancho La Brea are only 40,000 to 9,000 years old, the Rancholabrean Age represents the last 500,000 years of the Pleistocene Epoch.

Era	Period	Epoch	Millions of Years Ago
Cenozoic	Quaternary	Holocene	0.01
		Pleistocene	1.8
	Tertiary	Pliocene	5
		Miocene	24
		Oligocene	38
		Eocene	54
		Paleocene	65
Mesozoic	Cretaceous		145
	Jurassic		210
	Triassic		250
Paleozoic	Permian		290
	Carboniferous		365
	Devonian		415
	Silurian		465
	Ordovician		510
	Cambrian		575

Geologic Time

Available evidence indicates that our planet is about 4.6 billion years old. In order to discuss events that have taken place during the history of the earth, geologists have divided this span of time into smaller units called eras and epochs. The first 4 billion years of earth history saw the formation of the atmosphere, the seas, and the continents and the beginning of life. The Paleozoic Era, 575 to 250 million years ago, was a time of diversification of life in the oceans and exploitation of the land by primitive plants and animals. The Mesozoic Era (also known as the "Age of Reptiles"), 250 to 65 million years ago, was the time when dinosaurs roamed the earth and the flowering plants and birds and mammals first appeared. During the Cenozoic Era (or "Age of Mammals"), from 65 million years ago to the present, mammals replaced reptiles as the dominant large animals.

The Cenozoic Era is divided into a number of smaller units. The Tertiary Period comprises five epochs: the Paleocene (65 to 54 million years ago), the Eocene (54 to 38 million years ago), the Oligocene (38 to 24 million years ago), the Miocene (24 to 5 million years ago), and the Pliocene (5 to 1.8 million years ago). The Quaternary Period is composed of the Pleistocene epoch (1.8 million to 10,000 years ago) and the Recent or Holocene epoch.

Most of the animals and plants preserved as fossils in the Rancho La Brea deposits are from 10,000 to 40,000 years old. This interval of time, the latest part of the Pleistocene epoch, represents a very late stage in the history of the earth, about 65 million years after the last dinosaur died.

Radiometric Dating

All matter is composed of one or more chemical elements. Carbon, oxygen, nitrogen, and hydrogen are the most common elements in living organisms. Some elements are unstable when

The earth's 4.5 billion year history is depicted on the time ribbon mural in the Page Museum. Each inch of the 83-foot-long mural represents about five million years. The fossils from Rancho La Brea were formed from 40,000 to 9,000 years ago. They appear one one-hundredth of an inch (substantially less than the thickness of a sheet of paper) from the end of the ribbon.

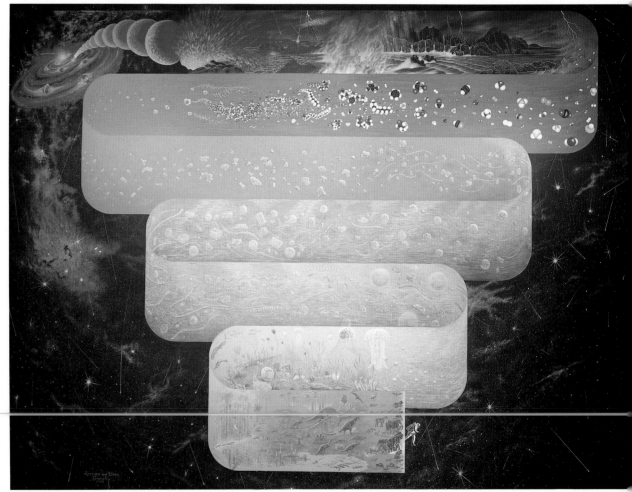

An imaginary slice through the layered sediments beneath Hancock Park shows how fossil deposits were formed as asphalt seepage and sediment deposition built up the land surface.

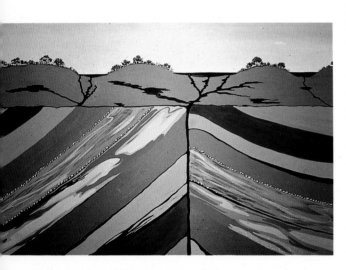

formed and change in time at a constant rate to more stable elements. It is this change that provides the basis for radiometric dating.

Although many different types of radiometric dating methods have been applied to Rancho La Brea materials, the most reliable technique is the carbon-14 analysis of bone material.

Bombardment of the upper atmosphere by cosmic rays results in the formation of a relatively constant amount of radioactive carbon (carbon-14) from the element nitrogen (nitrogen-14). As the carbon-14 spreads through the atmosphere it combines with oxygen to form carbon dioxide (CO_2), which is eventually absorbed by all living organisms.

The carbon dioxide that living organisms take in from their environment contains both normal carbon (carbon-12) and carbon-14 in a constant proportion. When a plant or animal dies, new carbon is no longer added to its tissues and the carbon-14 already present gradually changes back to nitrogen at a fixed and known rate. After 5,370 years, half the original carbon-14 will have been converted; this is known as the "half-life" of carbon-14. After another 5,370 years, half of the remaining carbon-14 (three fourths of the total carbon-14) will have been converted. After about 45,000 years, nearly all the carbon-14 will have reverted back to nitrogen. Thus the proportion of carbon-14 to carbon-12 in a dead organism can be used to calculate the length of time since the organism died. The radiocarbon dates for extinct animals from Rancho La Brea range from 11,000 to greater than 38,000 years.

The carbon-14 method can be used to date fossils directly, but it only works well for materials younger than 45,000 years. Materials older than this have to be dated by radiometric methods that involve other elements. The decay of

During the Pleistocene Ice Age, the western United States was covered with an extensive system of interconnected and isolated freshwater lakes (left); the climate today (right) is too dry for lakes to form.

radiometric potassium to argon is the most frequently used method. Unfortunately organic tissues contain a very small quantity of potassium, and so this method cannot be used to date fossils directly. Radiometric dates for fossils older than 50,000 years are usually estimated from potassium-rich rocks (such as volcanic lavas and ashes) found in the same layers of earth as the fossils.

Geologic History of the Area

One hundred thousand years ago, the area now occupied by Rancho La Brea lay beneath the surface of the Pacific Ocean. At the onset of the last glaciation of the Pleistocene Ice Age the sea retreated, exposing a flat plain between the edge of the ocean and the upstanding Santa Monica Mountains. Stream erosion of the Hollywood Hills resulted in the accumulation of large fan-shaped deposits of river sediment at the mouths of the canyons and extending out over the plain. Over the course of time, these alluvial fans extended farther from the mountains and raised the overall level of the plain.

Movement deep within the earth's crust resulted in the formation of cracks, faults, and fissures that cut through the layers of gravel, sand, and mud laid down by the streams and into the extensive natural reservoirs of the Salt Lake Oilfield. Crude oil seeped slowly upwards along these cracks until it reached the ground surface. At the surface the lighter petroleum portion evaporated, leaving behind shallow sticky pools of natural asphalt. Numerous asphalt seeps were once visible at Rancho La Brea; a few can still be seen in Hancock Park today. It is in such asphalt deposits that the Rancho La Brea fossils were preserved. The "tar pits" still visible in the park are the relics of some of the more than 100 sites excavated for asphalt and for fossils.

In 1926 Charles Knight, working under the direction of Chester Stock, painted this prehistoric scene of Rancho La Brea. Current research suggests that the area was less grassy and was covered by coastal sage brush with groves of pine, valley oak, and cypress.

The seeping of crude oil, which still continues today, has been going on for the past 40,000 years. Periodic outpouring of asphalt from fissures and vents continued as the alluvial plain was being built. Hard, oxidized asphalt lenses that formed at ground surface are now found buried beneath later sand and gravel deposits. Animals and plants were captured in shallow surface sheets of viscous asphalt rather than in large pools or "pits," but over time such asphalt layers built up into large conical bodies through continued deposition. The preservation of the bones and plant materials was aided by their subsequent burial in sediments of the alluvial plain.

The Environment of 40,000 Years Ago

Geologists, paleontologists, and biologists seek to understand the climate and ecology of the past using many different types of information. By comparing ancient sediments with those being

formed today, geologists are able to reconstruct the landscape of 40,000 years ago. By comparing the fossils with their nearest living relatives, biologists and paleontologists are able to understand more about ancient life. Differences between fossil animals and plants and their living representatives can tell us much about changes in climatic and environmental conditions at different times during the history of the earth.

We know from such studies that the Santa Monica Mountains, north of Hancock Park, also formed the horizon during the Pleistocene. Streams carried sediment and debris from the canyons and deposited them on the coastal plain. Fossil plants from La Brea indicate that the late Pleistocene climate was cooler and more moist and equable than our modern climate. Many of the plants or their closest living relatives occur today in the summer fog belt from San Luis Obispo north to Oregon and on California's Channel Islands. The slopes of the Santa

Monica Mountains were covered with chaparral, and redwood, dogwood, and bay occurred in deep, protected canyons. In the mountains and out onto the plain the stream courses were lined with sycamores, willows, alder, box elder, and live oak. Away from the stream courses, the plain was covered with coastal sage scrub punctuated by groves of closed-cone pine, valley oak, juniper, and cypress.

During the Pleistocene, therefore, although the shapes of the mountains and valleys would be familiar to the modern residents of Los Angeles, the climate was cooler and more humid, and the landscape was clothed by different kinds of vegetation and inhabited by some rather strange animals.

Preservation of the Fossils

Fossils are evidence of past life. Natural preservation of animals and plants can occur in many ways, but all require isolation from the effects of rapid decay. After an animal dies, its "soft tissues" (for example, flesh, skin, and hair) are scavenged or quickly decay. The harder parts of animals (bones and teeth, shells) tend to decay more slowly and are less likely to be destroyed by carnivores. A prerequisite for the preservation of bones, shells, and plants is rapid burial. For this reason, most fossils are found in sediments that accumulated in water (the deposits of ancient rivers, lakes, or oceans) where rapid burial can occur. The Rancho La Brea fossils appear to have been preserved by a unique combination of rapid sedimentation and asphalt impregnation.

Asphalt seeped to the surface through ancient stream channel deposits primarily during warm summer weather. The resulting shallow puddles were often concealed by a surface coating of leaves and dust. Occasionally, an

unwary animal became trapped by the asphalt and, in turn, lured a number of scavengers to their fate. The bodies soon decayed, individual bones rotted free, became saturated with asphalt and settled at least part way into the mire. During the winter, cool temperatures solidified the asphalt, and rainwater-choked streams deposited a layer of sediment over the exposed bones. The warm weather of early summer then dried the streams and liquefied the asphalt to reset the trap. Repetition of the annual cycle produced the cone-shaped bone masses found at Rancho La Brea.

As the asphalt becomes warm during the summer months it also becomes mobile. The movement of the asphalt within the deposit produces movement of the buried bones. As a result, bones from one skeleton may become separated and mixed with others. In fact, very few complete or articulated skeletons have been recovered from Rancho La Brea. In addition, bones that are moved around by the asphalt tend to rub against one another. Through time, this abrasion produces abnormal grooves and holes in the bones—a phenomenon known as "pit wear."

13

In 1914, a mass of fossil bones at the bottom of Pit 91 (left) was exposed and left in place as an exhibit. It later became covered over as the pit filled up with asphalt and debris.

Right: The fossil-bearing deposit at Pit 4, excavated in 1913, represents three cone-shaped asphalt bodies that have become joined together above the 20-foot level.

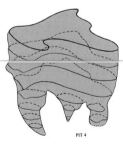

PIT 4

Pit 91 was reopened in 1969. One year later, excavation had revealed this densely packed mass of bones.

Excavation and Preparation Techniques

Most Rancho La Brea fossil deposits are large cone-shaped masses. The position of each bone in a deposit may provide clues to how the deposit was formed. Accordingly, during excavation the surface of a deposit is divided up by a grid into units 3 feet (0.9 meters) square, and each unit of the grid is excavated 6 inches (152 millimeters) at a time. The location of any fossil more than ½ inch (13 millimeters) long is recorded by a series of at least nine measurements to provide a three-dimensional record of its exact position and orientation within the deposit. Additional information is provided by photographs and sketches. The fossils are then carefully excavated with small hand tools: dental picks, trowels, and small chisels and brushes. Each fossil is placed with its excavation data into a separate container for further preparation and cataloging in the laboratory.

Large specimens are cleaned by hand in the laboratory. The sand, clay, and asphalt matrix is carefully removed. A solvent is used to dissolve the asphalt; the small or fragile specimens are cleaned in ultrasonic tanks, where high-frequency sound waves help the solvent to remove asphaltic sediment from the specimen. When the cleaning is completed, the specimens are rinsed and dried. The clean fossils are given a protective coating, identified, and assigned a catalog number, which is entered in a master catalog along with identification and locality data. Each specimen is then incorporated into the collections, where it will be available for further research.

After the large fossils have been removed from each grid unit at the excavation, the remaining sediment from each unit is placed in screen baskets and boiled in solvent to remove the asphalt. The cleaned material is a mixture of sand, small pebbles, and very small fossils (microfossils) including seeds and small plant remains, snails, insect parts (mostly beetle fragments), and bones and teeth of small vertebrates. The fossil remains are removed by hand under illuminated magnifiers and identified and cataloged.

Kinds of Fossils Recovered

Early excavators focused their attention on the bones of the larger and more spectacular mammals and birds and the larger pieces of fossil wood. The smaller mammals and birds, the invertebrates, and the seeds were rarely noticed or collected. Several decades later, workers began to retrieve fossil insects and other small fossils from the sediment or matrix inside some of the large mammal skulls.

15

In 1969, the staff of the Natural History Museum began a new excavation of Pit 91. Using modern, more sophisticated techniques, the new excavation sought to document how the fossiliferous deposits at Pit 91 were formed and to recover a greater diversity of fossils. The excavation has proved spectacularly successful in sampling a variety of previously uncollected small animals and plants. Many of the smaller sorts of La Brea fossils—seeds and pollen, insects and mollusks, fish, amphibians, and small birds and rodents—are best known from this excavation.

In all some 140 species of plants and more than 420 species of animals are now known from the Rancho La Brea deposits.

Scientific Names

There are many vernacular or common names for plants and animals, e.g., corn, dolphin, gopher, large-mouth black bass. Unfortunately, as in the first three examples listed, the same common name is sometimes applied to very different things. *Corn* could mean either wheat or maize. *Dolphin* has been used for a kind of fish and also for a small type of whale.

The common name *gopher* has been applied to rodents, a snake, and a tortoise. In other cases, many different common names have been used for the same species. The mountain lion is also known as the cougar or puma, and *large-mouth black bass* is only one of fifty-three common names applied to the fish whose scientific name is *Micropterus salmoides*.

A species is a single type of organism. The scientific name of a plant or animal species is a unique combination of two Latin words. The first word of the pair, which is always spelled with a capital letter, is the generic name (a genus consists of a group of closely related species). The second word is called the specific name. The international community of biologists has agreed that only one species of animal or plant may bear the same combination of names. Thus the extinct saber-toothed cat, *Smilodon californicus*, and the living black-tailed jackrabbit, *Lepus californicus*, have identical specific names, but each bears a unique combination of generic and specific names. The gray wolf, *Canis lupus*, and the extinct dire wolf, *Canis dirus*, are closely related and have the same generic name, but the second words of their scientific names identify them as different species.

Scientific names are precise and unambiguous. Moreover, many of the extinct animals and plants that paleontologists study have no accepted common names. In this book, we have provided the scientific name and, where possible, the common names of the fossil animals and plants from the Rancho La Brea deposits.

Reconstruction of Extinct Animals

The Rancho La Brea fauna is composed of both extinct and extant (still living) species. Some of the extant forms are still found in the southern California region: others no longer occur in the area. The extinct species were generally larger than modern forms. Comparing the extinct forms with their closest living relatives provides information on physiology and behavior. Some extinct species have no modern relative, and reconstructing the physical appearance of these animals requires a knowledge of the structure and function of their bones.

The initial stage of any reconstruction is to identify each of the animal's bones and to place the bones in their proper skeletal position. After the skeleton is assembled, the soft tissues can be modeled. Muscles sometimes leave distinct scars where they were attached to bones, and these can be used to estimate the size and proportions of the muscles. Hair, fur, and skin are rarely found in the fossil record, and so the external appearance (color and type of hair or feathers) of the extinct animal is usually based on those of modern relatives and structurally similar animals.

Animal Migrations between Continents

The composition of the North America fauna has changed greatly through time. Part of the change was due to the evolution of species on this continent. Other changes in the composition of the North American fauna resulted as animals migrated here from other continents. During the later part of the Cenozoic Era, faunal exchanges took place through two corridors.

The faunas of North and South America were isolated from each other until about 7 million years ago. At that time the first exchange of animals occurred across a volcanic island chain. Later, about 3.5 million years ago, the pace of faunal exchange increased as Central America emerged. The

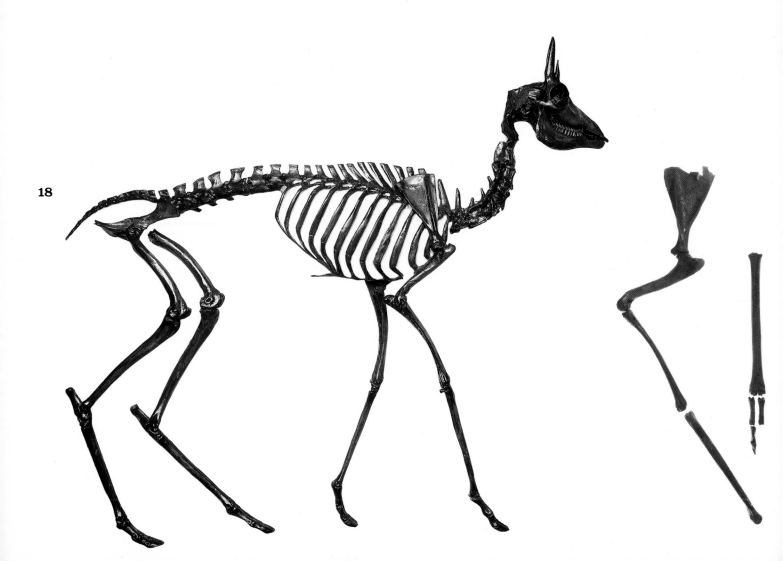

18

Reconstruction of fossil animals from Rancho La Brea is complicated by the fact that the individual skeletons of different species are jumbled together. Thus, the first step in the reconstruction of an extinct animal like the dwarf pronghorn is to isolate bones of this species and assemble those of individuals of the same size and age into a single skeleton. Next, the muscles and soft tissues are modeled in clay over the surface of the skull and skeleton. A cast of the model is then reproduced in plaster of Paris and painted. Comparisons with living relatives of the extinct animal provide clues to its appearance.

19

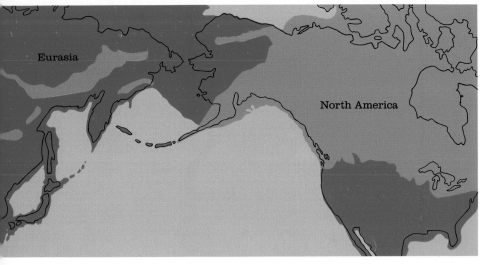

Eurasia

North America

Ice Age Continents Glaciers and Ice Sheets ＿＿＿ Today's Coastline

The Bering Land Bridge connected northeast Asia and northwestern North America during the Pleistocene glacial episodes. This connection provided a route for the migration and interchange of animals between the two continents.

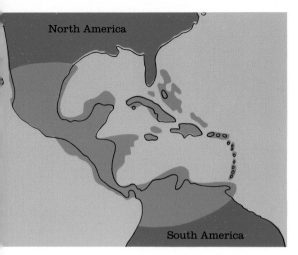

Ice Age Land Bridge

South America was isolated from North America for much of the Cenozoic Era but, beginning about 7 million years ago, the Central American Isthmus provided a corridor through which migration could take place in both directions.

ancestors of the ground sloths and the short-faced bear represented in the Rancho La Brea fauna came here from South America along this route. Similarly, rabbits, rodents, dogs, cats, horses, camels, and deer entered South America from the north.

Faunal exchange also occurred between North America and Eurasia during the Cenozoic across the Bering Strait, now a shallow sea separating Alaska and Siberia. Several times during the Pleistocene glaciations, sea level dropped, and the Bering "land bridge" emerged. This permitted species that evolved in North America, like the camel and horse, to migrate to Eurasia, while Eurasian animals like the mammoth, bison, and man entered North America.

Based on changes in the North American fauna resulting from a combination of evolution and migration, paleontologists have constructed a relative time sequence of successive mammalian faunas. These faunas have been used to characterize North American Land Mammal Ages. The Rancho La Brea fauna characterizes the Rancholabrean Land Mammal Age. The beginning of this time interval is defined as the first occurrence of bison in North America. The timing of such faunal changes has been determined by radiometric dating techniques.

21

Part 2

The Mammals

Over one million mammal fossils, representing at least fifty-nine different species, have been recovered from the asphalt deposits. Some species, particularly those of the larger carnivores, are represented by tens of thousands of bones and teeth. Other species (humans, tapirs, bats) are known only from a handful of specimens. The early collectors focused chiefly on the larger mammals. Our knowledge of the smaller forms (insectivores, rodents, etc.) is still far from complete.

24

Among the numerous human artifacts found in the younger Rancho La Brea deposits are (from upper left) bone and shell pendants, a wooden hairpin, and half of a basalt cogged stone of unknown function.

Human Remains

The remains of only one human, La Brea Woman, have been found in the Rancho La Brea deposits. A skull and partial skeleton were excavated in 1914. Carbon-14 tests indicate that the specimen is about 9,000 years old. Anatomical studies show that the fossil remains belonged to a woman who stood about 4 feet 10 inches tall (1.5 meters) and was between 20 and 25 years in age.

The skull of La Brea Woman was found in several pieces, the bones of the facial region being separated from those of the braincase. Parts of the skull are fractured. Some of the teeth had been lost before death and others show cavities and abcesses. Those teeth that still remain are extremely worn and indicate a diet of stone-ground meal.

Two theories have been proposed to explain the occurrence of this skeleton. It has recently been suggested that La Brea Woman was murdered by a blow to the head and her body dumped in a shallow tar pool. There is also some indication, from associated grave goods (a domestic dog skull and a deliberately damaged hand grinding stone or mano), that the skeletal remains may have been deliberately buried, as part of a ritual.

About one hundred human artifacts have been recovered from the younger La Brea deposits (less than 10,000 years in age). Seashells are the most common and were probably brought here for trade purposes. Some of these seashells were made into jewelry, some were used for domestic purposes (shell scoop). Other artifacts include hide scrapers made of elk horn from the southern San Joaquin Valley, bone and wooden hair pins, wooden spear tips, and several manos used to prepare flour.

Skull of La Brea woman and an artist's reconstruction of her.

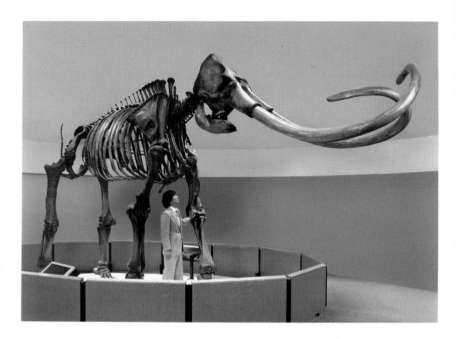

This mammoth skeleton, a composite of bones from several average-sized individuals, is about 12 feet tall.

Imperial Mammoth and American Mastodon

The imperial mammoth, *Mammuthus imperator*, was the largest of the elephants that lived in North America. Some individuals from Rancho La Brea stood over 13 feet (3.9 meters) tall. The average size adult was 12 feet (3.6 meters) tall and weighed about 10,000 pounds (4,900 kilograms).

Mammoths were closely related to the modern Indian and African elephants, and all three groups originated in Africa near the end of the Miocene epoch. Both Indian elephants and mammoths migrated out of Africa at the beginning of the Pliocene epoch, 5 million years ago, but only the mammoths reached the New World.

Elephants and mammoths have high-crowned teeth to cope with a diet of grass and other abrasive vegetation. The teeth are constructed of a series of vertical enamel plates, each with a core of dentine surrounded by a layer of cementum. Normally only four teeth are present in the mouth at any one time. As this set of teeth becomes worn, it is pushed forward and replaced by another set. This system of successive tooth replacement helps prolong the use of the teeth and enables modern elephants to live to an age of 60 years. When the final, sixth, set of teeth is worn out, the animal will die from starvation.

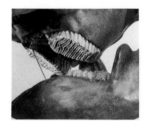

Mammoth teeth; the single upper molar, which is composed of a series of plates, is approximately 1 foot long.

Mammoths differed from living elephants by having a greater number of enamel plates in each individual tooth. Mammoths and elephants also differ in the shape of the tusks. Some mammoth species developed thick hairy coats to cope with cold arctic regions.

The American mastodon, *Mammut americanum*, which stood slightly more than 6 feet (1.8 meters) tall at the shoulder, was smaller than the imperial mammoth and also differed from it in a number of other features. Both possessed long elephantlike trunks, but mastodons had more teeth present in the jaw and, instead of tall plates, these had low rounded cusps separated by V-shaped valleys. The shape of the tooth crown suggests that mastodons fed on leaves and twigs rather than on the grass that provided the main item in a mammoth's diet.

Mastodons were only distantly related to the elephants. The earliest representatives of the mastodon family are known from Africa during the early part of the Tertiary Period, some 45 million years ago. They later migrated into Europe and Asia about 20 million years ago, reaching North America during the Middle Miocene, about 15 million years ago.

28

Page 28: American mastodon (left) and imperial mammoth.

Below: Skeleton of Harlan's ground sloth.

Ground sloths were large, primitive mammals related to the smaller, present-day tree sloths of Central and South America. Two types of ground sloths are common in the Rancho La Brea deposits, and a third is represented by a few specimens.

Harlan's ground sloth, *Glossotherium harlani*, stood a little over 6 feet (1.8 meters) tall and weighed about 3,500 pounds (1,570 kilograms). Its simple, flat grinding teeth indicate that it preferred a diet of grass, although it may also have fed on tubers, leaves, and twigs. These animals had nodules of bone, called dermal ossicles, embedded in the deeper layers of the skin of the neck and back. These may have served as protection against attack by predators.

The smaller Shasta ground sloth, *Nothrotheriops shastense*, had a tubular-shaped snout and fewer teeth than its larger relative. The structure of its teeth suggests that it was a browser, feeding on leaves from shrubs or low-hanging tree branches. Fossil dung from this beast, found in Arizona and Nevada, supports this view. A second, larger browsing ground sloth, *Megalonyx jeffersonii*, is rare at Rancho La Brea and represented by only a few specimens. Neither of the browsing species had the bony ossicles found in *Glossotherium harlani*.

Ground sloths originated in South America during the Oligocene epoch, 30 to 35 million years ago, before North and South America became joined by Central America. Ground sloths migrated to North America during the Late Miocene, 7 to 9 million years ago, where they survived until about 10,000 years ago.

Shasta ground sloth.

30

Harlan's ground sloth.

Horse and Tapir

The many horse bones recovered from the Rancho La Brea deposits belong to the extinct western horse, *Equus occidentalis*. Standing about 14½ hands (4 feet 10 inches, or 1.47 meters) high at the shoulders, this animal was as tall as a modern Arabian horse but more heavily built. The western horse had high-crowned cheek teeth with a complex pattern of resistant enamel. These provided an efficient grinding surface admirably suited for processing abrasive fodder.

The ancestry of horses can be traced back to the Cretaceous, although the first true horse, *Hyracotherium*, is known from the Eocene. *Hyracotherium* was about the size of a small dog, had four toes on the front foot and three toes on the hind foot, and had low-crowned teeth. During the course of time, horses became progressively larger and longer limbed. By the late Miocene, the ancestors of the western horse had evolved high-crowned check-teeth and had only a single functional toe on each foot. The evolutionary changes in the limbs and teeth were adaptations for living in an open, nonforested environment.

Known from the Eocene of both North America and Europe, horses subsequently became extinct in Europe during the Oligocene but persisted in North America, where they evolved rapidly. During the middle Miocene, three-toed horses dispersed from North America into Eurasia and Africa. On several occasions during the Pliocene and Pleistocene, one-toed horses migrated into Eurasia, Africa, and South America. Horses became extinct in North America at the end of the Pleistocene, but domestic horses were later reintroduced from Europe. The western horse from Rancho La Brea was one of the last species of horse native to North America.

Tapir.

Western horse.

The tapir, an interesting distant relative of the horse, is adapted for living in the dense vegetation surrounding swamps or in relatively thick forest. Tapirs have low-crowned teeth for browsing on leaves and other soft plant food, and their nose is modified into a short proboscis or "trunk," which is used to push food into the mouth. Like horses, they were formerly native to North America, Europe, and Asia. They were widespread in North America during the Pleistocene but disappeared at about the same time as the horse and are found today only in South America and Malaysia.

Although fossil tapir bones have been found at several sites in southern California, the only evidence for tapirs at Rancho La Brea consists of three small bones: two phalanges (toe bones) that were recovered in collections made by the University of California, Berkeley, and an ectocuneiform (bone from the ankle joint) from the Page Museum Collection.

This 1-inch-wide bone from the ankle joint has a distinctive shape that identifies it as tapir. It is one of three tapir bones found at Rancho La Brea.

Peccary

Zoologists divide the living swine into two families, the Suidae (pigs) of the Old World and the Tayassuidae (peccaries), now restricted to the New World. Peccaries occur today from the southwestern United States to Patagonia, but they were formerly more widely distributed and occurred as far afield as Kenya and South Africa. They differ from pigs in small but important details of the skull and teeth.

Right: The skull of the
extinct flat-headed
peccary is about 10
inches long. Below:
Flat-headed peccary.

Peccary remains in the Rancho La Brea
deposits include a partial skull and several foot bones of
Platygonus, the flat-headed peccary. This animal ranged widely
through the Americas during the Pleistocene epoch but now
occurs only in Paraguay. The Rancho La Brea peccary achieved
the size of the European wild boar and was somewhat larger than
its living North American relatives.

35

Camels

The camel family was represented at Rancho La Brea by two species, both now extinct. The larger and more common form, *Camelops hesternus*, stood more than 7 feet (2.1 meters) tall at the shoulder. It was of similar build to the living bactrian (two-humped) camel but had longer legs and may have lacked humps.

Also represented by a few limb bones and vertebrae is an extinct llama, *Hemiauchenia macrocephala*. Like the South American llamas, alpacas, and vicuñas, this creature had a long neck and slender legs but probably lacked a camel like hump. The species of *Hemiauchenia* from Rancho La Brea was about one-third larger than any living llama.

The earliest camels are from North American sites that have been dated at about 45 million years old. They subsequently migrated to Eurasia, Africa, and South America. *Camelops* was restricted in distribution to North America; however, *Hemiauchenia* was also present in South America. Today camels are native to Asia (bactrian camel) and North Africa (dromedary), and llamas occur only in South America.

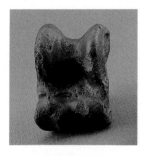

This 2-inch-long ankle bone of the extinct large-headed llama is one of the few specimens of this animal recovered from Rancho La Brea.

Deer and Pronghorns

Although deer are now the most abundant of the larger native animals of California, they are represented in the asphalt deposits by only a few individuals. The Rancho La Brea mule deer, *Odocoileus hemionus*, has cheek teeth adapted for chewing the leafy vegetation of bushes and trees and limbs modified for running and jumping through rough terrain.

Deer migrated to North America from Eurasia about 3 million years ago, during the late Pliocene. The remains of deer have been found at a number of other Pleistocene localities in California, and their rarity at Rancho La Brea suggests that the area was not a suitable deer habitat, or that

Western camel and large-headed llama.

37

Dwarf pronghorn.

Fossil skull of mule deer.

competition from larger herbivores might have restricted their numbers.

Pronghorns are often called antelopes but are only distantly related to the antelope and cattle of the Old World. They are solely North American in origin and distribution. Although represented today by a single species found only in western North America, pronghorns were more widely distributed during the Pleistocene. Two species of pronghorn have been recognized in the Rancho La Brea deposits. The larger Rancho La Brea species was very similar in size and appearance to the modern pronghorn, *Antilocapra americana*, but is known from only a few specimens. Much more abundant are the remains of a dwarf pronghorn, *Capromeryx minor*, which stood less than 2 feet (0.6 meter) tall at the shoulder and differed from *Antilocapra* in having horns with two distinct prongs arising from their base.

The horns of the pronghorn are retained throughout the life of the animal but are covered by a horny sheath that is shed annually. Members of the pronghorn family (Antilocapridae) may, in this way, be distinguished from other horned mammals, such as the true antelopes and cattle (whose unbranched horns are not shed), giraffes (whose "horns" are covered with skin), and deer (whose branched antlers are shed annually).

Bison and Musk-Oxen

Bison are the most common large herbivores in the Rancho La Brea fauna. They are represented by two extinct species, both larger than the modern bison, or "buffalo." *Bison latifrons*, the long-horned bison, had a 6-foot (1.8-meter) spread of horns and was larger but less common than *Bison antiquus*, the ancient bison.

**Long-horned bison
(left) and ancient bison.**

Bison belong to the cattle family
(Bovidae), and their earliest fossil record is from Eurasia. Bison
migrated across the Bering Strait into North America about half
a million years ago.

Although musk-oxen have not been found
in the Rancho La Brea deposits in Hancock Park, a site of similar age located only ten blocks from the park has yielded
remains of a musk-ox, *Eucheratherium*. This group of bovids is
more closely related to sheep than to cattle. Musk-oxen are today
restricted to Greenland and the Arctic region of North America
but formerly ranged as far afield as South Africa.

Dire wolf.

Dogs

Representatives of the dog family (Canidae) are the most abundant animals from the Rancho La Brea deposits. The most common species is the dire wolf, *Canis dirus*, known from the bones of more than 1,600 individuals. It is thought that packs of dire wolves attempted to feed on animals trapped in the asphalt and while doing so became mired themselves.

The dire wolf was similar in size to the closely related gray wolf, *Canis lupus*, which is also found at this site. The dire wolf had a massive head with strong jaws, large teeth, and legs that were proportionately shorter than those of the gray wolf.

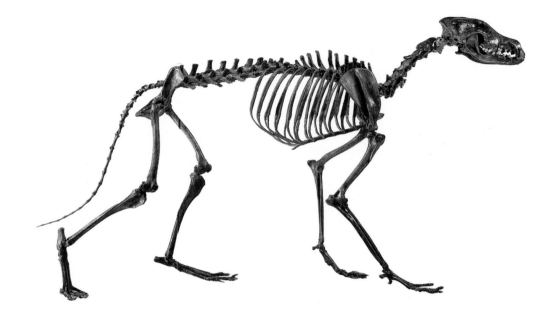

Fossil coyote skeleton (above) and fossil gray fox skull.

Coyotes, *Canis latrans*, are the third most abundant mammal species from the Rancho La Brea deposits. The fossil specimens are slightly larger than coyotes found in the area today. Fossil specimens of the living gray fox, *Urocyon cinereoargenteus*, have been recovered in small numbers. Two different types of domestic dog have been recovered from the younger levels of the deposit.

The dog family is one of the oldest groups of modern carnivores; earliest representatives are from the Eocene epoch of North America. Fifty genera of doglike mammals are known from the Tertiary period. Most of them were adapted for running swiftly in pursuit of their prey.

Bears

Three different types of bears have been found in the Rancho La Brea deposits. The most common is the short-faced bear, *Arctodus simus*. This is a large extinct species that was limited to North and South America. It had unusually long legs and was taller than the Kodiak bear from Alaska, although it was less heavily built. Most bears are opportunistic feeders, and their teeth have been modified to cope with a diet that includes both meat and vegetation. The short-faced bear, however, more closely retained the primitive carnivore tooth pattern and may have eaten more meat than its living counterparts. The only living relative of the short-faced bear is the spectacled bear, *Tremarctos ornatus*, from South America.

Fossil badger skull.

Other bears represented at Rancho La Brea are the black bear, *Ursus americanus*, and the grizzly bear, *Ursus arctos*. The black bear was present, though uncommon, throughout the Rancho La Brea sequence; the grizzly bear is known only from the younger levels.

Bears evolved from doglike ancestors during the Miocene epoch. Originally they had a carnivorous diet, but they subsequently adopted a mixed and mainly herbivorous diet. Although the earliest bears are from Europe, they are known to have occurred in North America from the beginning of the Pliocene epoch.

Weasels and Raccoons

The smaller carnivores from Rancho La Brea are all living today. The weasel, *Mustela frenata*, was the most common and is represented by more than fifty skulls. Other members of the weasel family (Mustelidae) known from the asphalt are the striped skunk, *Mephitis mephitis*, the spotted skunk, *Spilogale putorius*, and the badger, *Taxidea taxus*. All appear to have been somewhat larger than their living counterparts.

Short-faced bear.

The weasel family has a fossil record of over 30 million years, extending back into the Oligocene epoch. However, as is often the case with small forest-dwelling animals, the few known fossil remains are very fragmentary. Badgers and skunks are known from the Miocene epoch onward.

Two members of the raccoon family (Procyonidae), the ring-tailed cat, *Bassariscus astutus*, and the raccoon, *Procyon lotor*, are now known from the Rancho La Brea deposits. Both are very rare. This group appears to have originated in North America during the Miocene epoch but had radiated into Eurasia and South America by the beginning of the Pliocene epoch.

Front portion of a fossil jaguar skull; the canine tooth is about 2 inches long.

Cats

The largest cat from the asphalt deposits is the American lion, *Panthera atrox*. This extinct species strongly resembled the African and Asian lions in features of the teeth and skeleton. Female American lions were the size of African lions, but the males were about 25 percent larger. Pumas are represented by two species, the living puma, *Felis concolor*, and the extinct *Felis daggetti*, which was a little larger. The bobcat, *Lynx rufus*, from the Rancho La Brea deposits resembles the species still found in California. Bobcat bones are not common at Rancho La Brea, but those found vary sufficiently in size to suggest a slightly larger extinct variety may also have been present. The jaguar, *Panthera onca*, is also represented, although rare, in the Rancho La Brea deposits. The fossil jaguar is slightly larger than the living form.

Members of the cat family (Felidae) were among the earliest of the modern carnivores to appear in the fossil record and are known from the late Eocene epoch onward.

American lion and California saber-toothed cat.

Most of the early felids had long saber-like canines; the modern cat-like forms with short canines did not appear until the Pliocene epoch. It is entirely possible that the "normal" modern cat tribe evolved from ancestors with long canines.

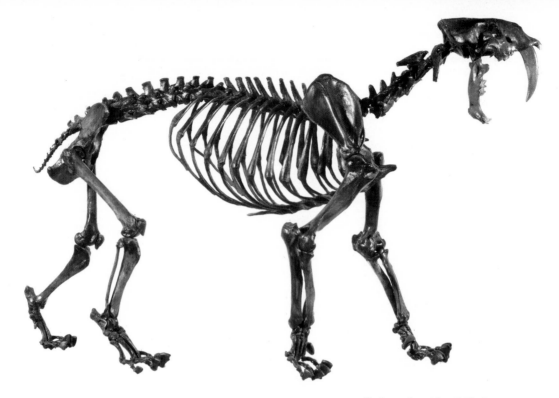

**California saber-
toothed cat skeleton.**

Saber-toothed Cat

Of all the animals known from Rancho La Brea, *Smilodon californicus*, the saber-toothed cat species, most vividly captures the imagination. It has been named the state fossil of California. *Smilodon* is the second most common fossil from the asphalt deposits (next to dire wolves). It was the size of the modern African lion. The very powerful limbs indicate that the saber-toothed cat used stealth and ambush rather than speed to capture its prey. Nevertheless, saber-toothed cats could probably attain a speed of 25 to 30 miles (40 to 48 kilometers) per hour in short bursts.

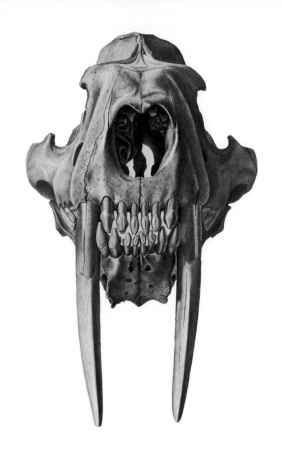

The function of the large upper canine teeth has been debated for decades. Their knifelike shape coupled with powerful muscles for lowering the head have led many scientists to believe the canines were used to stab or slash large prey animals. However, a recent investigation suggests instead that the saber-toothed cat probably used its canines to bite open the soft underbelly of its prey.

Some paleontologists believe that the saber-toothed cats were social animals, living and hunting in packs that provided food for old and infirm members. Many of the saber-toothed cat bones recovered from Rancho La Brea show evidence of arthritis and other bone disease.

Saber-toothed cats, which are classified in a separate subfamily from true cats, first appeared in the Eocene epoch. They were prominent members of the faunas of North America and the Old World from the Oligocene epoch until the end of the Pleistocene epoch and may have given rise to true cats during the Pliocene epoch.

California saber-toothed cat skull, shown at about one-third actual size. From *The Felidae of Rancho La Brea* by J.C. Merriam and C. Stock, Courtesy of Carnegie Institution of Washington.

Fossil valley pocket gopher skull.

Fossil California pocket mouse skull.

Fossil desert cottontail rabbit skull.

Small Mammals

The early excavators at Rancho La Brea were primarily interested in the large extinct animals and collected very few of the smaller remains. Even so, much of the information about the small fossil mammals comes from research on the earlier collections. Most of the species of small mammals found in Rancho La Brea deposits are still living today, and many might still be found in the vicinity were it not for the urban expansion that has taken place during the past half century.

Insectivores are represented by the ornate shrew, *Sorex ornatus*, and the desert shrew, *Notiosorex crawfordi*. Both are known from several specimens. The broad-handed mole, *Scapanus latimanus*, is known from a limb bone and pelvis. Insectivores are among the most primitive of living mammals, and their ancestry can be traced back over 70 million years into the Cretaceous period.

Two species of bat have been recorded from the asphalt deposits. The hoary bat, *Lasiurus cinereus*, is known only from the end of one limb bone. A smaller, as yet undetermined species is also represented by one limb bone. Bats had evolved from insectivore ancestors by the early Eocene epoch, but their delicate bones are seldom found as fossils.

Rodents are much more common in Rancho La Brea material than bats or insectivores. Represented species include Beechey's ground squirrel, *Spermophilus beecheyi*, the Pacific kangaroo rat, *Dipodomys agilis*, the California pocket mouse, *Perognathus californicus*, the valley pocket gopher, *Thomomys bottae*, the California meadow mouse, *Microtus californicus*, the southern grasshopper mouse, *Onychomys torridus*, the western harvest mouse, *Reithrodontomys megalotis*, a packrat of the genus *Neotoma*, and a deer mouse, *Peromyscus imperfectus*.

The origin of the rodents is obscure. It is presumed that they evolved from a primitive insectivore stock; they are first recorded from the late Paleocene epoch, 60 million years ago. The squirrels are a specialized offshoot from the most primitive rodent group. In contrast, rats and mice are usually considered the most advanced types of rodents.

The fossil remains of three types of rabbits have been recovered from Rancho La Brea: the brush rabbit, *Sylvilagus bachmani*, the desert cottontail, *Sylvilagus audubonii*, and the black-tailed jackrabbit, *Lepus californicus*. Rabbits and hares belong to an order (Lagomorpha) that is distantly related to other types of mammals. The modern forms, including those from Rancho La Brea, have descended from a stock first known from Oligocene deposits of Eurasia.

49

Black-tailed jackrabbit.

Part 3

The Birds

The number of bird bones recovered from Rancho La Brea is particularly noteworthy. The bones of birds, like those of most small animals, are rare in fossil deposits because their delicate structure reduces chances for preservation. At Rancho La Brea, however, the asphalt provided a protective coating for the bones of birds that became trapped. The Rancho La Brea deposits have yielded the largest collection of fossil birds from anywhere in the world, totaling more than 100,000 cataloged specimens. Over 135 bird species, nineteen of which are extinct, have been identified.

Many of the birds represent carnivorous and scavenging species that may have been inadvertently trapped in the asphalt while attempting to feed on other trapped animals. Water birds may have landed in or near asphalt pools, mistaking them for water. Although the fossil birds include a number of these species (herons, ibises, ducks, geese, plovers, and sandpipers, for example), they make up only a small percentage of the total. This suggests that the asphalt deposits were not located in or near the permanent standing bodies of water that were probably present in the area.

52

Eagles and Falcons

More than twenty species of eagles, hawks, and falcons have been found at Rancho La Brea. The eagles include both species found today in North America: the Golden Eagle, *Aquila chrysaetos*, and Bald Eagle, *Haliaeetus leucocephalus*. The Golden Eagle is the most common fossil bird with more than 950 individuals represented. Also present were extinct species, such as Woodward's Eagle, *Amplibuteo woodwardi*, the Fragile Eagle, *Buteogallus fragilis,* and Grinnell's Crested Eagle, *Spizaetus grinnelli*, that have no living representatives and whose relatives are now confined to Central and South America. Perhaps the most interesting fossil eagle is *Wetmoregyps daggetti*, whose legs were as long as those of a Great Blue Heron, *Andes herodias*.

Falcon remains include those of the Prairie Falcon, *Falco mexicanus*, Peregrine Falcon, *Falco peregrinus*, Merlin, *Falco columbarius*, and Kestrel, *Falco sparverius*. Also present was an extinct species of Caracara, *Polyborus prelutosus*, a ground-dwelling carrion feeder.

Pages 52 and 53
from left to right:
Woodward Eagle,
Fragile Eagle, La Brea
Caracara, and
Grinnell's Crested
Eagle.

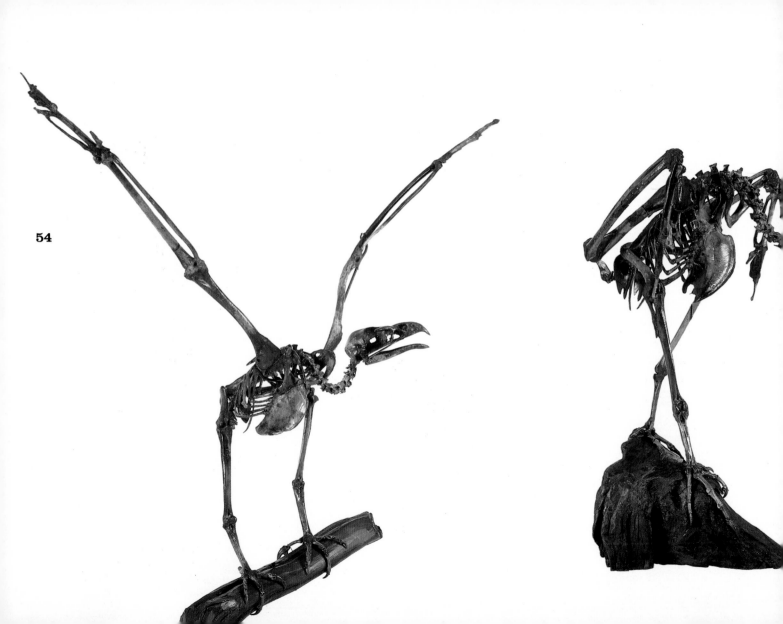

54

From left to right: Errant Eagle, Occidental Vulture, and Brea Condor.

Condors and Vultures

The nearly extinct California Condor, *Gymnogyps californianus*, is the largest living terrestrial bird in North America. Its immediate ancestor, *Gymnogyps amplus*, was present in the Rancho La Brea fauna. Although attributed to a separate species, the ancestral condor can be distinguished from the living form by only minor differences in the skull and by its slightly larger size. Also present was another extinct condor, *Breagyps clarki*, that was slightly smaller than the California Condor and had a longer, more slender beak. A third extinct species, the Western Black Vulture, *Coragyps occidentalis*, is closely related to the living Black Vulture, *Coragyps atratus*, of western North America. Remains of the living Turkey Vulture, *Cathartes aura*, are also found in the asphalt deposits.

       The condors and vultures presently living in North America are not closely related to the Old World vultures, although both have adopted a scavenging mode of life. The New World vultures are, in terms of living birds, most closely related to the storks; the Old World vultures are close relatives of the eagles. Two species of Old World vultures are found in the La Brea deposits, the American Neophron, *Neophrontops americanus,* and the Errant Eagle, *Neogyps errans.*

55

56

Teratorns, Storks, and Turkeys

The largest bird from the asphalt deposits belongs to the extinct family Teratornithidae, which is related to storks and New World vultures. Remains of more than 100 individuals of Merriam's Teratorn, *Teratornis merriami*, which weighed about 30 pounds (13 to 14 kilograms) and had a wingspan of about 14 feet (3.2 meters), have been recovered. The similarity in appearance between the bones of teratorns and condors led early researchers to believe that both were scavengers. More recent research indicates that teratorns were active predators, stalking their prey on the ground and then swallowing them whole. It is probable that teratorns trapped in the asphalt were seeking their prey around the fringes of the asphalt deposits.

The tallest bird in the Rancho La Brea fauna is a stork, *Ciconia maltha*, that stood about 4½ feet (1.4 meters) high. This species is the most common representative of the stork family at this site.

The second most common species of bird found in the asphalt deposits is an extinct species of turkey, *Meleagris californica*, which was slightly smaller than but otherwise similar to the living Ocellated Turkey of Yucatan, Mexico. Many of the bones of this species are from young birds. Broods of turkey chicks tend to stay together; if one were caught in the asphalt, its cries of distress would attract the remainder of the brood, who might in turn become trapped. Thus it is possible that the social behavior of the turkeys resulted in entire family groups being trapped at one time.

Owls, Woodpeckers, and Songbirds

Nine different kinds of owls, including one extinct species, are found at Rancho La Brea. The most abundant species is the Burrowing Owl, *Speotyto cunicularia*, but there are almost as many specimens of the Barn Owl, *Tyto alba*. The Great Horned Owl, *Bubo virginianus*, was also very common. Generally nocturnal hunters, the owls were probably trapped while trying to prey on small animals struggling to free themselves from the asphalt.

Woodpeckers are not common in the Rancho La Brea fauna, but at least seven species were preserved in the asphalt deposits. Most abundant is the Common Flicker, *Colaptes auratus*.

Many specimens of songbirds, or passerines, are preserved in the Rancho La Brea deposits, but their small bones are extremely difficult to identify with accuracy. Over thirty-five species have been identified so far, the most common being the Yellow-billed Magpie, *Pica nuttalli*, Common Raven, *Corvus corax*, and Western Meadowlark, *Sturnella neglecta*.

Reptiles, Amphibians and Fish

Part 4

Top to bottom: western
skink, western rattle-
snake, and western
toad.

Seven different lizard species have been identified: the desert **59**
spiny lizard, *Sceloporus magister*, the western fence lizard,
Sceloporus occidentalis, the side-blotched lizard, *Uta
stansburiana*, the coast horned lizard (horny toad), *Phrynosoma
coronatum*, the southern alligator lizard, *Gerrhonotus
multicarinatus*, the whiptailed lizard, *Cnemidophorus tigris*,
and the western skink, *Eumeces skiltoneanus*.

Nine snake species are known: a racer,
Coluber constrictor, the gopher snake, *Pituophis melanoleucus*,
the common king snake, *Lampropeltis getulus*, two garter
snakes, *Thamnophis couchi* and *Thamnophis sirtalis*, the
striped racer, *Masticophis lateralis*, the ringneck snake, *Dia-
dophis punctatus*, and the western rattlesnake, *Crotalus viridis*.
Abundant remains of the western pond turtle, *Clemmys
marmorata*, have also been found.

Five species of amphibians have been re-
corded from the asphalt deposits: the western toad, *Bufo boreas*,
the southwestern toad, *Bufo microscaphus*, the red-legged frog,
Rana aurora, a tree frog, *Hyla regilla*, and a climbing salaman-
der, *Aneides lugubris*. Remains of toads are much more common
than those of frogs.

60   Three-spined
          stickleback.

All the amphibian and reptile species occur today in southern California. The presence of the frogs and the pond turtle indicate permanent bodies of water in the area and suggest that the climate was a little more humid than at present.

Remains of three species of fish have been recovered from Rancho La Brea: the rainbow trout, *Salmo gairdnerii*, the arroyo chub, *Gila orcutti*, and the three-spined stickleback, *Gasterosteus aculeatus*. The type of stickleback found in the asphalt deposits is less heavily armored than most representatives of the species, and both this unarmored form of stickleback and the chub are restricted to the Los Angeles Basin. In contrast, the rainbow trout is native to western North America and is found in coastal drainages from Alaska to Baja California. All the trout fossils were fish less than 5 inches (125 millimeters) in length. The chub remains are of fish from 2.5 to 3 inches (60 to 80 millimeters) long, and the sticklebacks were from 1.5 to 2.5 inches (40 to 60 millimeters) long. When found together, remains of these three fish indicate that there were permanent, slowly flowing streams in the area.

Only four other freshwater fish species are known from the Los Angeles Basin. Two are lampreys and lack bony elements that might be preserved as fossils. The other two fish, the speckled dace, *Rhinichthys osculus*, and Santa Ana sucker, *Catostomus santaanae*, are found in upper stream courses in the San Gabriel Mountains; their absence from the asphalt deposits suggests that the ancient streams that flowed through Rancho La Brea were of local origin with headwaters in the Santa Monica Mountains.

The Invertebrates

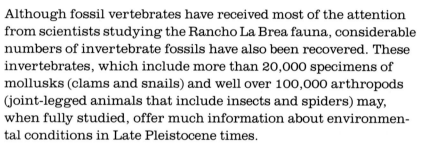

Top: Dragonflies trapped on the surface of a present-day asphalt seep in Kern County, California. Bottom: A blow fly pupa (arrow) fossilized in a dire wolf jaw.

63

Although fossil vertebrates have received most of the attention from scientists studying the Rancho La Brea fauna, considerable numbers of invertebrate fossils have also been recovered. These invertebrates, which include more than 20,000 specimens of mollusks (clams and snails) and well over 100,000 arthropods (joint-legged animals that include insects and spiders) may, when fully studied, offer much information about environmental conditions in Late Pleistocene times.

Freshwater mollusks are represented by two species of clam and five species of snail. The aquatic mollusks suggest the presence of ponds or streams through at least part of the year. Interestingly enough, the only species of land snail from the asphalt deposit is found today not in California but only on high rocky slopes in Arizona, New Mexico, and Baja California: these snails were probably washed downstream from the Santa Monica Mountains. Shells of marine mollusks are common in the deposits that underlie the vertebrate fossil horizons, but the only marine mollusks associated with vertebrate fossils were brought there by humans.

Seven different orders of insects have been found—grasshoppers and crickets, termites, true bugs, leafhoppers, beetles (the most abundant because their hard bodies preserve well), flies, and ants and wasps. Other arthropods are represented by millipedes, scorpions, several families of spiders, ostracods ("water fleas") and isopods (sow bugs or pill bugs).

Some of the fossilized insects, especially the bugs and beetles, were aquatic and would have been preserved naturally in stream or pond deposits. However, more than half of the represented species lived on land and are only infrequently found as fossils. Some of the beetles and flies were carrion feeders and may thus have become trapped while feeding on carcasses of animals that were stuck in the asphalt; the other kinds of insects were probably trapped when they were blown into, or inadvertently crawled over, the sticky asphalt.

Although early workers on La Brea insects identified many extinct species, modern studies indicate that nearly all of the fossilized specimens represent insects that are still living today (although some, because of climatic change, are no longer found in the Los Angeles area). The only two extinct species now recognized from Rancho La Brea are dung beetles. These beetles are dependent on plentiful supplies of dung for their life cycle, and their extinction might have coincided with that of the larger mammals at the end of the Pleistocene.

Jerusalem cricket
(*Stenopelmatus
fuscus*), a large,
ground-dwelling insect
found fossilized in Ran-
cho La Brea deposits.

The Plants

Part 6

California lilac.

Fossil plant material from Rancho La Brea consists of wood, leaves, cones, seeds, and microscopic remains (pollen and diatoms). Well over 100,000 plant fossils have been recovered. Some of the material is from plants that lived in the immediate area, and some shows evidence of being transported by flood waters or streams. Studies of the plant material and late Pleistocene landscape have suggested that four plant associations were present in the area.

The slopes of the Santa Monica Mountains were covered with chaparral. Chaparral can be characterized as being composed of tall, usually densely packed, deeply rooted, woody bushes that are dependent on fire for vitality. Although probably not much different in appearance than today, the chaparral of Pleistocene times was composed of many plants that no longer occur in the region. The dominant plants of this association included chamise, lilac, scrub oak, manzanita, walnut, elderberry, coffeeberry, and poison oak. Juniper and digger pine were probably scattered in the chaparral in more open, drier areas. Coast live oak probably occurred in groves on north-facing slopes, in smaller canyons, and on the lower slopes of deeper canyons.

A second group of plants, including coast redwood, bay, and dogwood, occurred in the largest deep, protected canyons. The presence of this association in the Santa Monica Mountains probably represented its southernmost prehistoric distribution. These plants probably grew in proximity to coast live oak and stream bank (riparian) plants.

The plants that inhabited stream margins and springs form a third association. Along the mountain streams, this group included sycamore, alder, arroyo willow, dogwood, raspberry, poison oak, and numerous herbs. Where the streams crossed the plain, the association consisted of arroyo willow, red cedar, occasional coast live oak, sycamore, elderberry, walnut, numerous herbs, and possibly bishop pine.

The typical coastal sage scrub association is composed primarily of small, drought-tolerant, woody bushes that are openly spaced, allowing room for herbs and grasses. In Pleistocene times, this association, punctuated by valley oak and groves of closed-cone pine, covered the plain. The dominant plants of this association included coastal sage brush, black sage, and buckwheat. Subordinate plants included saltbush, tarweed, ragweed, thistle, morning glory, several annual herbs, and a few grasses. Manzanita and juniper also occurred frequently in this association. Valley oaks were scattered at higher elevations on the alluvial fans. Groves of Monterey cypress and Monterey pine occurred in favorable sites on the plain.

Chaparral and grove of coast live oak. Photograph by David Minor.

Scientific Name	Common Name	Scientific Name	Common Name
Chaparral Association		*Acer negundo*	box elder
Adenostoma fasciculatum	chamise	*Salix lasiolepis*	arroyo willow
Ceanothus species	lilac	*Cornus californica*	dogwood
Quercus agrifolia	coast live oak	*Rubus vitifolius*	raspberry
Quercus dumosa	scrub oak	*Toxicodendron diversilobum*	poison oak
Arctostaphylos species	manzanita	*Juniperus* species	red cedar
Juglans californica	walnut	*Sambucus mexicana*	elderberry
Sambucus mexicana	elderberry	*Quercus agrifolia*	coast live oak
Rhamnus californica	coffeeberry	*Juglans californica*	walnut
Toxicodendron diversilobum	poison oak	*Pinus muricata*	Bishop pine
Pinus sabiniana	digger pine		
Juniperus californica	California juniper	**Coastal Sage Scrub Association**	
Deep Canyon Association		*Artemisia* species	coastal sage brush
Sequoia sempervirens	coast redwood	*Salvia* species	sage
Umbellularia californica	California bay	*Eriogonum* species	buckwheat
Cornus californica	dogwood	*Atriplex* species	saltbush
		Hemizonia fasciculata	tarweed
Stream Margin and Spring Association		*Ambrosia* species	ragweed
Platanus racemosa	sycamore	*Cirsium* species	thistle
Alnus rhombifolia	alder	*Convolvulus* species	morning glory

The Future: Questions Remain

Part 7

The study of the Rancho La Brea fossils is still far from complete. **71**
Most of the initial identifications of the different types of fossils
have been made, but detailed investigation of the plants, invertebrates, birds, and small mammals is still in progress. When
completed, such studies will provide much more precise information about the past climate and environment of the region.

At present, we know that the Rancho La
Brea fossils range in age from 4,000 to nearly 40,000 years.
Documentation of the exact age of each concentration of fossils
will provide further information about evolutionary changes
that took place during this interval of time. Investigations of the
ways in which the deposits were formed are still in progress.
These will in turn help us understand how the fossils came to be
preserved in the asphalt and, perhaps, why there are so many
examples of some animals but so few of others.

Proportions of Herbivores to Carnivores

Ecologically, life can be viewed as a pyramid, with a broad base of
plants that use inorganic elements and the sun's energy for
growth. Herbivores, animals that eat plants, are much less abundant than plants and make up the middle of the pyramid. At the

Carnivora 90%

 Badger*

 Fox*

 Puma

 American Lion

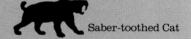 Saber-toothed Cat

 Short-faced Bear

Weasel*

Artiodactyla 5% Camel Pronghorn Peccary

Perissodactyla 2.5% Tapir

Edentata 2% Ground Sloths Horse

Proboscidea 0.5% Imperial Mammoth

 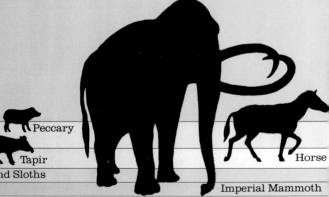

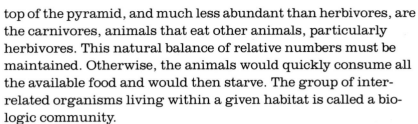

top of the pyramid, and much less abundant than herbivores, are the carnivores, animals that eat other animals, particularly herbivores. This natural balance of relative numbers must be maintained. Otherwise, the animals would quickly consume all the available food and would then starve. The group of inter-related organisms living within a given habitat is called a biologic community.

Fossil assemblages may or may not represent an accurate cross section of a prehistoric biologic community. An unbiased sample of such an assemblage should contain many more herbivores than carnivores. This, however, is not the case at Rancho La Brea: carnivores far outnumber herbivores. A **73** plausible explanation is that single herbivores and packs of carnivores pursuing them both inadvertently became trapped in the asphalt and that scavengers attracted to these carcasses also became trapped. An event of this nature, resulting in the entrapment of perhaps ten animals, need only have happened once every decade over an interval of 30,000 years to account for the number and proportion of the animals fossilized at Rancho La Brea. Further excavation and continuing research will provide additional information to help explain the abnormal percentage of carnivores in the Rancho La Brea collections.

Chart showing the relative proportions of the different types of mammals found in the Rancho La Brea depos- its. Predatory forms (Carnivora) predominate. Percentages are approximate values.

*Similar to living species

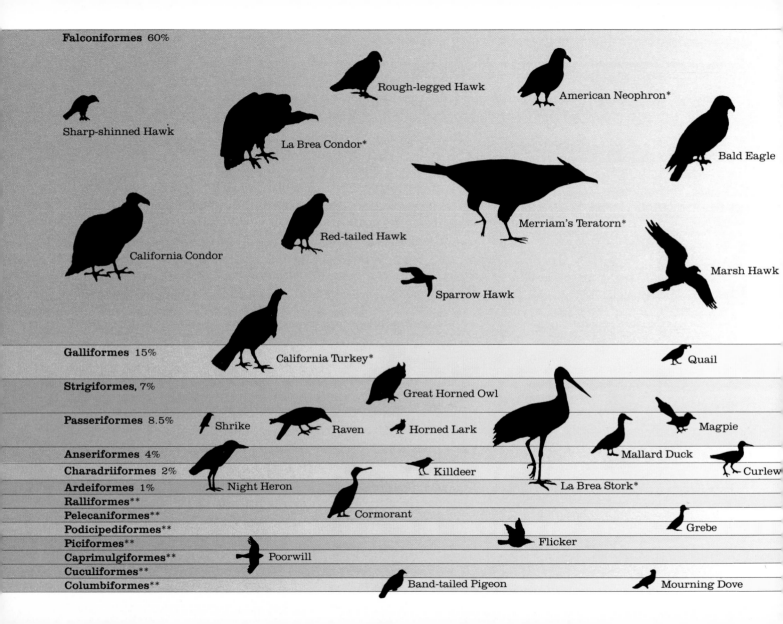

Falconiformes 60%

Sharp-shinned Hawk

Rough-legged Hawk

American Neophron*

La Brea Condor*

Bald Eagle

California Condor

Red-tailed Hawk

Merriam's Teratorn*

Marsh Hawk

Sparrow Hawk

Galliformes 15%

California Turkey*

Quail

Strigiformes, 7%

Great Horned Owl

Passeriformes 8.5%

Shrike

Raven

Horned Lark

Magpie

Anseriformes 4%

Mallard Duck

Charadriiformes 2%

Killdeer

Curlew

Ardeiformes 1%

Night Heron

La Brea Stork*

Ralliformes**

Pelecaniformes**

Cormorant

Podicipediformes**

Grebe

Piciformes**

Caprimulgiformes**

Flicker

Poorwill

Cuculiformes**

Columbiformes**

Band-tailed Pigeon

Mourning Dove

Grinnell's Crested Eagle*

Prairie Falcon

La Brea Caracara*

Daggett Eagle*

Golden Eagle

La Brea Owl*

Canada Goose

Avocet

Crane

Roadrunner

Extinctions

Animals become extinct if they are unable to cope with changes in the prevailing environmental conditions, if they are unable to compete successfully with other animals for available food sources, or if through disease and predation their breeding population falls below a critical minimum number. Many of the large mammals from Rancho La Brea are now extinct. Evidence from other localities suggests that these animals died out between 8,000 and 11,000 years ago. The reasons for their extinction have been the subject of considerable debate.

Humans were present in the New World shortly before most of the late Pleistocene large mammals became extinct, and human predation has sometimes been proposed as the cause of the extinctions. Humans have certainly contributed to a drastic decline in wildlife species in historic times by enclosing and modifying land for agricultural and building purposes and by excessive hunting. However, it seems less likely that small numbers of early humans in the New World,

75

Chart showing the relative proportions of the different types of birds found in Rancho La Brea deposits. As in the mammals, carnivorous forms (Falconiformes, some Passeriformes, and Strigiformes) dominate. Percentages are approximate values.

*Extinct Species
**Less than 1%

Feet

0   5

lacking sophisticated weapons and following a hunter-gatherer existence, could have significantly affected the local large animal populations.

An alternative explanation is that major climatic shifts at the end of the Pleistocene epoch resulted in vegetation changes that affected the large herbivores and the large carnivores that preyed upon them. However, it is possible that, through hunting, humans could have assisted in the demise of those New World species already adversely affected by climatic and vegetational change.

The Importance of the Fossils

The Rancho La Brea fossil deposits provide a spectacularly comprehensive record of life in the Los Angeles region toward the end of the Pleistocene Ice Age. The preservation of many of the specimens is unusually complete, permitting detailed studies of the form and function of animals that are long extinct. The deposits even preserve plant fragments in the teeth of some of the larger herbivores, thus providing a sample of what these animals were eating just before they died.

The importance of the fossils recovered from Rancho La Brea, and of the deposits that remain in and around Hancock Park, cannot be overestimated. They hold the key to resolution of many current and future questions about the surroundings in which the first human immigrants to North American found themselves.

Did the early inhabitants of North America hunt mammoths and other large land mammals into extinction?

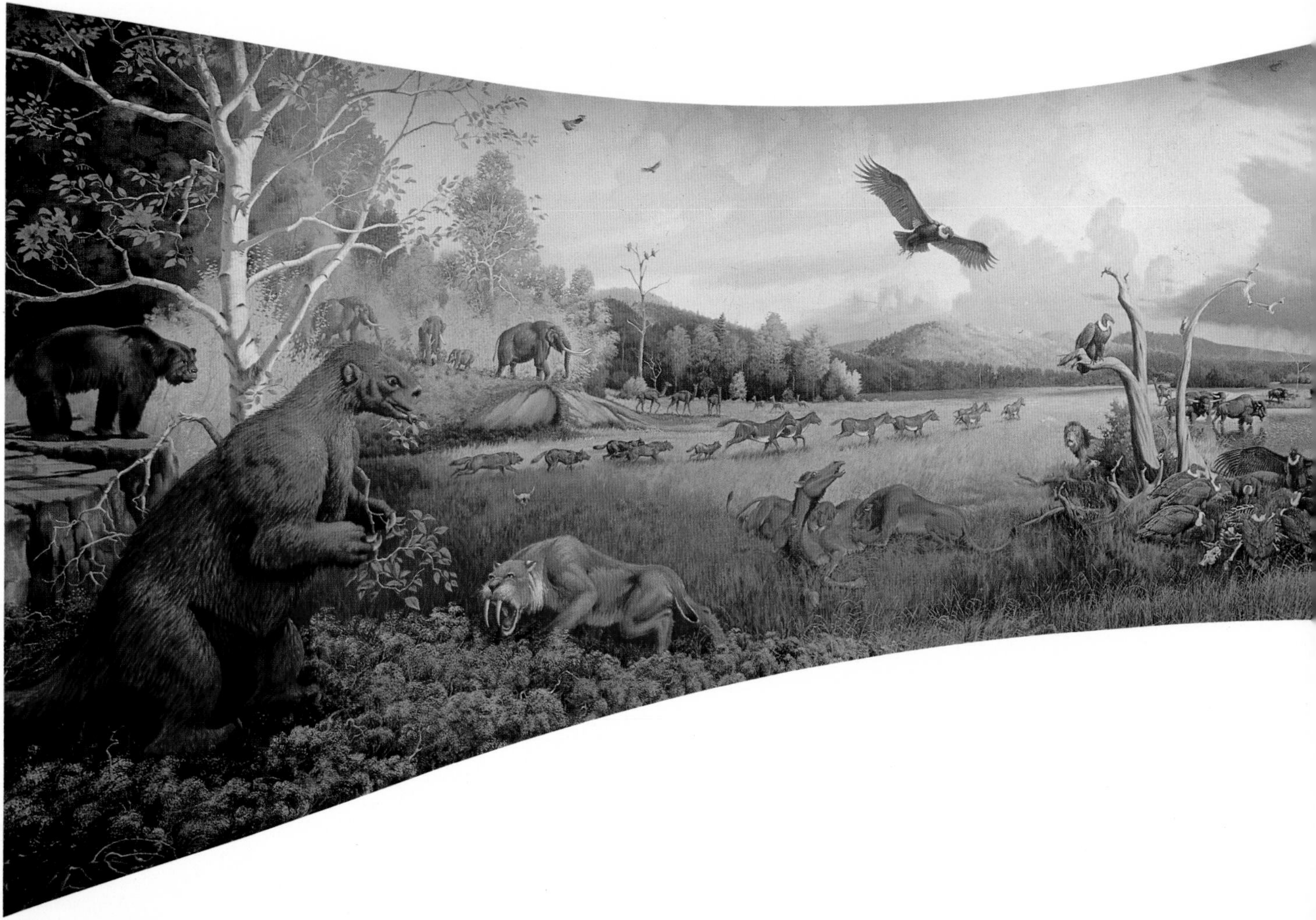

Hancock Park Today

Named for the philanthropic founder of the Los Angeles based Mission Pak Company, the Page Museum in Hancock Park first opened its doors to the public on April 13, 1977, after nearly two years of construction. The Page Museum was built to house the Rancho La Brea heritage of over one million specimens of fossil plants and animals. In presenting that heritage, the museum features over thirty different exhibits of skeletons, murals and paintings, and historic photographs as well as an introductory multimedia presentation and several films. The museum also has a glass-walled laboratory and offices where curatorial activities and research are carried out by members of the staff of the Natural History Museum of Los Angeles County.

A mural in the Page Museum showing extinct mammals and birds whose remains have been found in the Rancho La Brea deposits and elsewhere in southern California.

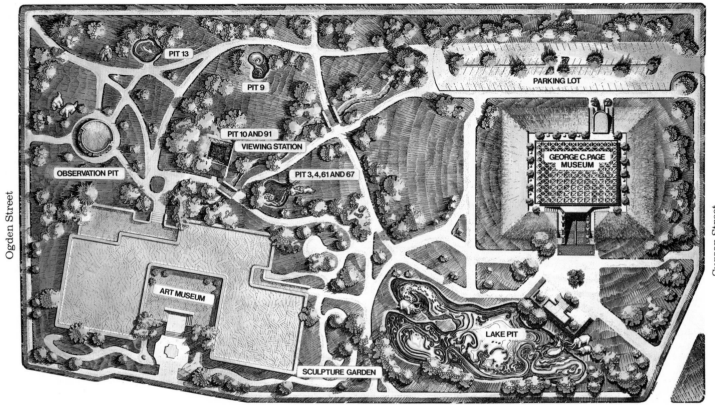

PIT 13

PIT 9

PARKING LOT

PIT 10 AND 91

VIEWING STATION

OBSERVATION PIT

PIT 3, 4, 61 AND 67

GEORGE C. PAGE
MUSEUM

Ogden Street

Curson Street

ART MUSEUM

LAKE PIT

SCULPTURE GARDEN

Wilshire Boulevard

**A bird's eye view of
Hancock Park.**

The Observation Pit at the west end of Hancock Park, which first opened in 1952, is a circular building that surrounds a partially excavated deposit of fossils and bubbling asphalt.

In 1963, Rancho La Brea was designated a National Natural Landmark by the National Park Service.

82 The "fish bowl" laboratory in the Page Museum allows visitors to watch curatorial activities. Steps in preparing a fossil include, from left to right, cleaning the specimen, identifying it by comparing it with other material in the collections, and cataloging the specimen; at far right, microfossils, including bones of birds and small mammals and plant and insect material, are sorted under a magnifying lens.

 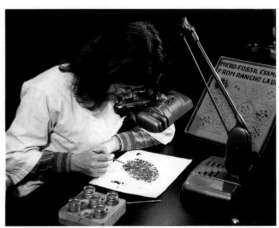

Akersten, W.A. 1985. *Canine Function in* Smilodon. Contributions in Science, no. 356. Natural History Museum of Los Angeles County.

Akersten, W.A., C.A. Shaw, and G.T. Jefferson. 1983. Rancho La Brea: Status and Future. *Paleobiology* 9(3):211-17.

Bromage, T.B., and S. Shermis. 1981. The La Brea Woman (HC 1323): Descriptive Analysis. *Occasional Papers of the Society for California Archaeology* 3:59-75.

Campbell, K.C., and E.P. Tonni. 1983. Size and Locomotion in Teratorns (Aves: Teratornithidae). *The Auk* 100:390-403.

Gray, R. 1983. *Giants from the Past: The Age of Mammals*. Washington, D.C.: National Geographic Society.

Howard, H. 1962. *A Comparison of Prehistoric Avian Assemblages from Individual Pits at Rancho La Brea*. Contributions in Science, no. 58. Los Angeles County Museum.

Kurten, B., and E. Anderson. 1980. *Pleistocene Mammals of North America*. New York: Columbia University Press.

Marcus, L.F. 1960. *A Census of the Abundant Large Pleistocene Mammals from Rancho La Brea*. Contributions in Science, no. 38. Los Angeles County Museum.

Marcus, L.F., and R. Berger. 1984. The Significance of Radiocarbon Dates for Rancho La Brea. In *Quaternary Extinctions*, edited by P.S. Martin and R.G. Klein, 159-83. Tucson: University of Arizona Press.

Martin, P.S., and R.G. Klein, editors. 1984. *Quaternary Extinctions*. Tucson: University of Arizona Press.

Merriam, J.C., and C. Stock. 1932. *The Felidae of Rancho La Brea*. Carnegie Institute of Washington Publication 422.

Miller, S.E. 1983. Late Quaternary Insects of Rancho La Brea and McKittrick, California. *Quaternary Research* 20:90-104.

Miller, W.E. 1971. *Pleistocene Vertebrates of the Los Angeles Basin and Vicinity (Exclusive of Rancho La Brea)* Science Bulletin, no. 10. Natural History Museum of Los Angeles County.

Nowak, R.M. 1979. *North American Quaternary* Canis. Museum of Natural History, University of Kansas, Monograph 6.

Shaw, C.A. 1982. Techniques Used in Excavation, Preparation, and Curation of Fossils from Rancho La Brea. *Curator* 25:6377.

Stock, C. 1925. *Cenozoic Gravigrade Edentates of Western North America with Special Reference to the Pleistocene Megalonychinae and Mylodontidae of Rancho La Brea*. Carnegie Institute of Washington Publication 331.

——. 1956. *Rancho La Brea: A Record of Pleistocene Life in California*, 6th edition. Science Series 20. Los Angeles County Museum of Natural History.

Warter, J.K. 1976. Late Pleistocene Plant Communities—Evidence from the Rancho La Brea Tar Pits. In *Plant Communities of Southern California*, edited by J. Letting, 32-39. Berkeley, Calif.: California Native Plant Society (Special Publication 2).

Woodard, G.D., and L.F. Marcus. 1973. Rancho La Brea Fossil Deposits: A Re-evaluation from Stratigraphic and Geological Evidence. *Journal of Paleontology* 47:54-69.

Index

87